Amazing Plant Bodies
Tiny to Gigantic

by Ellen Lawrence

Consultants:

Suzy Gazlay, MA
Recipient, Presidential Award for Excellence in Science Teaching

Dr. Robin Wall Kimmerer
Professor of Environmental and Forest Biology
SUNY College of Environmental Science and Forestry, Syracuse, New York

Kimberly Brenneman, PhD
National Institute for Early Education Research, Rutgers University
New Brunswick, New Jersey

BEARPORT
PUBLISHING

New York, New York

Credits

Cover, © Bournemouth News & Picture Service; 3L, © kkaplin/Shutterstock; 3R, © Teerapun/Shutterstock; 4, © Mark Moffett/Minden Pictures/FLPA; 5, © Mark Newman/FLPA; 6T, © Filipe B. Varela/Shutterstock and © Mayovskyy Andrew/Shutterstock; 6BL, © Anna Kucherova/Shutterstock; 6BC, © Belinka/Shutterstock; 6BR, © Vaclav Volrab/Shutterstock; 7, © Ambient Images Inc/Superstock; 8L, © craftvision/istockphoto; 8, © Filipe B. Varela/Shutterstock and © Mayovskyy Andrew/Shutterstock; 9, © Reinhard Dirscherl/FLPA; 10–11, © Imagebroker/FLPA; 11BR, © Jim Brandenburg/Minden Pictures/FLPA; 12, © Wayne P. Armstrong; 13, © Bournemouth News & Picture Service; 15, © Radek Detinsky/Alamy; 15R, © Frans Lanting/FLPA; 16B, © Tamara Kulikova/Shutterstock; 16R, © Charles Marden Fitch/Superstock; 17T, © Werner Lang/Imagebroker/FLPA; 17R, © Stockfolio 704/Alamy; 18, © Vinicius Tupinamba/Shutterstock; 19, © Sabena Jane Blackbird/Alamy; 20, © Viktar Malyshchyts/Shutterstock; 21, © Boston Globe/Getty Images; 22L, © Igor Dutina/Shutterstock; 22R, © Mayovskyy Andrew/Shutterstock; 23TL, © Imagebroker/FLPA; 23TC, © Bogdan Wankowicz/Shutterstock; 23TR, © motorolka/Shutterstock; 23BL, © Tom Biegalski/Shutterstock; 23BC, © leungchopan/Shutterstock; 23BR, © Charles Marden Fitch/Superstock.

Publisher: Kenn Goin
Editorial Director: Adam Siegel
Creative Director: Spencer Brinker
Design: Elaine Wilkinson
Photo Researcher: Ruby Tuesday Books Ltd

Library of Congress Cataloging-in-Publication Data

Lawrence, Ellen, 1967–
 Amazing plant bodies : tiny to gigantic / by Ellen Lawrence.
      p. cm. — (Plant-ology series)
 Includes bibliographical references and index.
 ISBN 978-1-61772-592-0 (library binding) — ISBN 1-61772-592-7 (library binding)
 1. Plant size—Juvenile literature. 2. Stems (Botany)—Morphology—Juvenile literature. I. Title.

QK641.L39 2013
 581.4'95—dc23

                          2012019348

For more information, write to Bearport Publishing Company, Inc., 45 West 21st Street, Suite 3B, New York, New York 10010. Printed in the United States of America.

10 9 8 7 6 5 4 3 2 1

Contents

An Amazing Discovery

In 2006, scientist Steve Sillett climbed a very tall redwood tree.

At the top of the tree, he held one end of a tape measure to the tree's tip.

He let the other end drop to the ground.

Hundreds of feet below Steve, another scientist recorded the redwood's height.

The tape measure showed the tree was just over 379 feet (116 m) tall.

Steve had just climbed the tallest tree in the world!

Steve Sillett climbing a giant redwood tree

a redwood tree

The redwood tree that Steve climbed in 2006 is named Hyperion. At that time, it was the tallest tree in the world. In the future, however, an even taller tree might be discovered. Hyperion grows in Redwood National Park in California.

Statue of Liberty
305 feet 6 inches
(93 m) tall

Hyperion
379 feet (116 m) tall

Giant Plants, Tiny Plants

Plants can be tall, like a redwood tree, or short, like a daisy.

Whatever their size, most plants have the same parts.

They have roots that usually grow down into the soil.

They also have stems that connect their roots to their leaves.

Many plants also have flowers that make **seeds**, and some plants grow fruits.

All these plant parts come in many different shapes and sizes.

flower

leaf

stem

roots

sunflower plant

People eat the different parts of many plants. Which plant parts are these foods?
(The answers are on page 24.)

carrot

lettuce

apple

Giant sequoia (sih-KWOI-uh) trees have very thick stems, or trunks. A sequoia named the General Sherman tree has a huge trunk. It would take more than 20 adults holding hands to make a circle around its trunk.

trunk of General Sherman tree

Underground Plant Parts

The roots of most plants grow underground.

Roots take in water and **nutrients** from the soil.

They also hold a plant in place and keep it from falling over.

Some plants, such as sunflowers, have lots of roots that spread out in the soil.

Others, such as carrot plants, have one main root called a taproot.

taproot →

spreading roots →

mangrove roots

Most roots grow underground from the bottom of a plant's stem. Some mangrove plants, however, have roots that grow out of their stems, above the ground. Mangroves grow in water on seashores.

mangrove roots

Super Stems

A plant's stem carries water and nutrients from the roots to the rest of the plant.

The stems, or trunks, of baobab (BAY-uh-bab) trees can grow to be very fat.

These trees grow in hot, dry **deserts** where it may not rain for up to nine months!

When rain does fall, the tree stores gallons of water in its trunk, ready for the dry times.

The trunk of a large baobab tree can hold enough water to fill 50 bathtubs!

EUROPE

ASIA

Pacific Ocean

AFRICA

Indian Ocean

N
W · E
S

Madagascar

AUSTRALIA

■ Where baobab trees grow

baobab tree

Bamboo is a type of grass that grows in Asian countries such as China and Japan. One type of giant bamboo has the fastest-growing stems of any plant. Its stems can grow as much as three feet (1 m) in one day!

trunk

giant bamboo stem

Leaves Make Food

A plant's leaves make the food it needs for **energy** and to help it grow.

Leaves do this using water, a **gas** from the air called carbon dioxide, and sunlight.

Whether they are huge or tiny, all leaves can make food.

One type of pygmy weed plant has some of the smallest leaves in the world.

Each tiny leaf is the size of a pinhead.

a close-up view of pygmy stonecrop leaves

pinhead

actual size of pygmy stonecrop leaves

pinhead

gunnera plant leaf

Some of the biggest leaves in the world grow on gunnera (GUHN-ur-uh) plants. One gunnera plant grew a leaf that was 11 feet (3.4 m) wide!

Go on a leaf hunt. Find the biggest and smallest leaves growing in a park or in your schoolyard. Use a ruler to measure them. Then draw the leaves in a notebook.

The Biggest Flower

Many plants grow flowers.

The biggest flower in the world grows on a **rain forest** plant called a rafflesia (ruh-FLEE-zhuh).

A huge flower bud opens into a giant flower that can be three feet (I m) wide!

The flower makes tiny seeds inside small fruits called berries.

People who live where rafflesia flowers grow call them corpse flowers. The giant flowers got this name because they smell like a dead, rotting body, or corpse!

The rafflesia plants with the biggest flowers grow in rain forests on Borneo and Sumatra, which are islands in Asia.

ASIA

Pacific Ocean

Borneo

Sumatra

Indian Ocean

N
W E
S

AUSTRALIA

rafflesia
flower bud

rafflesia flower

Seeds Make New Plants

A seed can be as tiny as a speck of dust or bigger than a football.

Inside every seed is all the material needed to grow a new plant.

The tiniest seeds in the world belong to a type of orchid plant.

If 300 of these seeds were laid end to end, they would only measure one inch (2.5 cm) long.

orchid seeds

orchid flower

The biggest and heaviest seeds in the world come from the coco de mer palm tree. Each of the tree's giant seeds can weigh up to 40 pounds (18 kg).

coco de mer palm tree

Coco de mer palm trees grow wild on the Seychelles Islands.

ASIA

AFRICA

Seychelles Islands

Atlantic Ocean

Indian Ocean

N W E S

coco de mer seed

A Super-Sized Fruit!

Some plants grow their seeds inside fruits, which help protect the seeds.

A fruit can be small, like a blueberry, or big, like a watermelon.

The jackfruit tree produces the largest tree-growing fruits in the world.

A jackfruit can be 3 feet (1 m) long and weigh 100 pounds (45 kg).

That's as heavy as 320 baseballs.

Each giant jackfruit may contain up to 500 seeds.

seeds

jackfruit

There's one very large fruit that grows on the ground and can be even heavier than a jackfruit. People buy this fruit at Halloween. Can you guess what it is?

The outside of a jackfruit smells like rotting onions. The inside, however, tastes like a mixture of bananas and pineapples.

jackfruit

Amazing Plant Bodies

There are hundreds of thousands of different plants in the world.

Some have stems that are taller than 35-story skyscrapers.

Others have seeds that are almost too small to see.

The roots, stems, leaves, flowers, seeds, and fruits of plants all have important jobs to do.

From tiny to gigantic, plant bodies are growing, producing food, and making seeds that will grow into new amazing plants.

Giant pumpkins are the largest fruits in the world. People take part in contests to see who can grow the biggest one. Just one of these huge pumpkins can weigh more than 30 second graders!

pumpkin

seed

giant
pumpkins

21

Science Lab

Grow Giant Sunflowers

Did you know that giant sunflower plants can grow to be more than 20 feet (6 m) tall?

Plant some giant sunflower seeds and keep a record of how the plants grow.

Measure your plants every week and write down how tall they are.

How high did the tallest plant grow?

How wide was the biggest flower?

Draw one of the plants and label its parts.

Look for seeds growing in the centers of the flowers.

How to grow your sunflowers

Ask a grown-up to help you buy giant sunflower seeds online or from a garden center.

1 Packages of seeds have directions telling you when and how to plant them. Plant your sunflower seeds in potting soil in flowerpots or Styrofoam cups (with holes punched in the bottom).

2 Place the containers in a sunny window.

3 Water the seeds to keep the soil moist.

4 Soon tiny seedlings will appear.

5 When your plants are about three inches (7.6 cm) tall, plant them in a garden or in a large container.

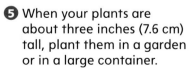

6 If the soil gets dry, water your plants.

Science Words

deserts (DEZ-urts) dry areas with few plants and little rainfall; deserts are often covered with sand or rocks

energy (EN-ur-jee) the power needed by all living things to grow, develop, and stay alive

gas (GASS) matter that floats in air and is neither a liquid nor a solid; most gases, such as carbon dioxide, are invisible

nutrients (NOO-tree-uhnts) substances needed by plants to grow and stay healthy; most plants take in nutrients from the soil using their roots

rain forest (RAYN FOR-ist) a warm place where many trees grow and lots of rain falls

seeds (SEEDZ) parts of a plant that can grow into new plants

Index

Read More

Bash, Barbara. *Tree of Life: The World of the African Baobab.* San Francisco: Sierra Club Books for Children (2006).

Charman, Andy. *I Wonder Why Trees Have Leaves, and Other Questions About Plants.* Danbury, CT: Grolier (2005).

Souza, D. M. *Wacky Trees.* New York: Scholastic (2003).

Learn More Online

To learn more about amazing plant bodies, visit
www.bearportpublishing.com/Plant-ology

About the Author

Ellen Lawrence lives in the United Kingdom. Her favorite books to write are those about nature and animals. In fact, the first book Ellen bought for herself, when she was six years old, was the story of a gorilla named Patty Cake that was born in New York's Central Park Zoo.

Answers

Page 6: A carrot is the root of a plant. Lettuce is a type of leaf. An apple is a fruit.

24

3 1170 00897 5082